SEBASTIAN WARRICK

PRIVATE LABEL SECRETS

The Ultimate Guide on How to Earn Money
Using PLR, Get a Step-by-Step Guide on How to
Profit Using Private Label Rights Products

Descrierea CIP a Bibliotecii Naţionale a României
SEBASTIAN WARRICK
PRIVATE LABEL SECRETS. The Ultimate Guide on How
to Earn Money Using PLR, Get a Step-by-Step Guide on How
to Profit Using Private Label Rights Products / Sebastian
Warrick – Bucharest: Editura My Ebook, 2021
    ISBN

SEBASTIAN WARRICK

PRIVATE LABEL SECRETS

**The Ultimate Guide on How to Earn Money
Using PLR, Get a Step-by-Step Guide on How to
Profit Using Private Label Rights Products**

My Ebook Publishing House
Bucharest, 2021

TABLE OF CONTENTS

INTRODUCTION

One of the best things about selling online is that it can often mean you get to 'skip' a lot of the grunt work that is normally involved in designing and selling a product. That means that you can avoid having to create a product from scratch, having to spend thousands on marketing campaigns, or having to manufacture physical goods. It has *never* been easier for anyone to decide they want to start making money and then begin making sales from the comfort of their own home.

While there are many business models that allow for this kind of 'fast tracked' success, few can rival the impressive speed and efficiency of selling private label rights products and as we'll see, this is a business model that can start earning you money in *days* (or less!). Not only that, but this is a business model that requires no technical skills and that anyone can use. There is no need for programming, video editing or even advanced search engine optimization.

Sound too good to be true? Well in this case, it really *is* that good! Here's how it works...

Essentially a private label rights product is a product for which you have the full rights. That means that it is yours to do with completely as you please and the only difference between a PLR product and one you make yourself is that it won't be exclusive.

You find the product you want to sell, you pay just once and then you sell it as your own. In addition, you'll be able to make any changes you see fit, put your own name on it, choose the price... as far as your customers are aware, this is a product that you made entirely yourself and they will have no knowledge of the involvement of any third parties!

In using this method, countless savvy entrepreneurs around the world are making an absolute killing by selling products that are designed by professionals to sell like crazy. With no need for those people to write their own books, edit their own videos... even put together their own marketing materials... this is literally a 'cut and paste' business model that is simple to implement and almost fool-proof in execution.

What You Will Learn

Sound good? Then keep reading to discover everything you could possibly ever need to know about PLR. You'll learn how to choose the best PLR products that will be guaranteed to sell in large numbers. You'll discover how you can edit and customize your products to better fit your brand image and to increase your sales, and you'll learn to market and promote your products to bring more sales to your business.

Here's just a few of the specific things you will discover throughout this book:

- Where to find the best PLR products

- What different types of licenses mean and what you need to look for

- How to pick the right products that will sell the best

- How to customize products to help them fit your brand

- How to face competition that is selling the exact same thing!

- How to set up your sales page

- How to process orders

- How to build a mailing list

- How to scale your business

- And much more!

Are you ready to start creating your own highly profitable income model in just a few simple steps? Then read on!

Chapter 1

What is Private Label Rights (PLR)?

To recap, PLR means that you get the full rights to edit and distribute a product. There is no need to credit the original author, all profits are entirely your own and you make changes wherever you see fit.

Of course, you will first need to buy the product from a seller before you can start doing this. The seller will be someone who is good at content creation but perhaps doesn't want to do their own marketing. Either that, or they'll already be selling the products themselves and they'll simply see this as another way to start making extra cash from something they've already created (by also selling to marketers and charging a little more to give them the full rights). The creator can continue to sell their own book, so they are not losing anything by making additional sales in this way; especially if they sell mainly through their own list and so are unlikely to be going into direct competition with others.

From your perspective, this means that you can buy a ready- made product and go about selling it as you please.

Except it's generally even better than that. Normally, you'll find that the creator *also* packages in a lot of other extras to help you sell. That means they might provide you with a 'ready-made' sales page, ready-made email marketing messages... ready-made freebies that you can give away with your product and more!

The products themselves can also vary but they will generally be *digital* products. That means the product is something intangible that provides value by offering information. The most classic and obvious example is selling eBooks, which are simply large, book- length documents saved in PDF format (in most cases).

Other options, however, can include courses, video courses, audiobooks, software, reports etc.

Likewise, a PLR product can of course focus on nearly any niche, whether that be fitness, making money online, dating, or something else entirely. In any case, the best strategy is to look for a niche that you are interested in, or better yet, one in which you already have established yourself as an authority.

Why You Should be Excited About PLR

So why is this so exciting? Why should you be eager to start getting involved with PLR products?

The first and most obvious advantage of PLR is that you won't have to make the products yourself. If you want to sell a 20,000- word eBook for instance, then all you need to do is to find the book you like and then place a 'buy now' button on your website.

This means you don't need to be a fantastic writer, it means you don't need to spend days or months writing a book, and it means that you don't need to handle things like editing the front cover or formatting the layout.

What's more, is that the end product you'll get to sell is likely to be more professional than whatever you could create yourself. That is not to undermine your skills as a creator but simply to state that a PLR product is a product that has been designed and created from the ground up by a team of experts (or an individual expert…); by people who do this for a living and who know the market well.

These are people who have access to all the most useful tools for creating products and who know how to put something together that will get a response from audiences. This, of course, increases the likelihood that your product will sell and it improves your chances of getting a positive response from those who buy it.

Better yet is the fact that even your *sales materials* are ready- made for you. And once again, these are ready made by people who truly understand the business and know how to write highly effective sales content that will help you to sell quickly and effectively.

Another benefit from not having to create the product yourself is that you'll be able to scale much more easily and you'll be taking far less risk.

If you create a product on your own or even commission the creation of a product, then you will need to spend either countless hours of your own time *or* a lot of money in getting the product created. If your product then turns out to be a failure and no one buys it, you will have *lost* all of that time and all of that money.

How long before you try again?

Even if the product is a success, you'll then need to go back to the drawing board in order to rebuild your *new* product and get it to the point where it is ready to sell. This will make it hard for you to really capitalize on your initial successes, and it will mean you could end up taking a long time to follow up and build on that initial success.

Compare this with selling PLR products. Here, you can launch a product and quickly start making big sales and then follow that up almost immediately with a new product. You can then pour the profits from that into two new products or three – quickly and effectively scaling up your business for massive profit.

Likewise, if you buy a PLR product and start selling it and it doesn't go right, then you haven't lost much. A PLR product won't set you back by that much in most cases and because you didn't have to invest huge amounts of time, you can simply pick up the pieces and then try again!

Even *more* powerful is the fact that you can choose products that you already know are selling well. That in turn, means that you can 100% guarantee that the products at least have the *potential* to sell well. They're already selling and the only thing that is changing is the website they are selling from. You are literally lifting someone's tried and tested business and then dropping it onto your site.

There has never been a more straightforward way to make money, or one that offers better odds for you as the seller!

Types of Rights

Before you jump in, one of the first things you need to consider is the type of rights that you are going to be buying. This is important as getting it wrong could mean that you can't actually sell the product, or you can't edit it – the latter point may or may not be an issue depending on your intended business strategy.

There are a few different terms you need to familiarize yourself with in that case. These are:

Resale Rights / Resell Rights (RR) Master Resale Rights (MRR) Private Label Rights (PLR) Personal Use Rights Public Domain

And more.

Let's take a look at each.

First of all, **resale rights** (RR), mean that you have the right to resell the product. This is pretty straightforward and does precisely what it says on the tin. However, this does not necessarily mean that you'll be able to make edits to the product. You may be able to but in that case, you have additional rights *on top* of the resale rights and you need to check that this is explicitly stated. In most cases, you'll also gain access to some of the sales materials that the creator has been using to sell their products. In this way, you are being actively encouraged to sell!

Master resale rights (MRR) meanwhile means that you not only have the right to resell the product but you also have the right to resell the rights. In other words, you can resell the product to *other marketers* so that they can resell it as well! This creates another avenue for you to sell through and is especially useful if you happen to be in the internet marketing niche – in which case, most of your potential customers will probably be interested in selling as well. Once again, however, you will still not necessarily have the right to edit the original documents/files.

Private Label Right (PLR) is where the product becomes *truly* yours and without limit. Now you can not only sell the product *and* the rights but you also have the option to edit the product. That means you can put your name on it, you can put your company's brand on it, or you can even change the very topic of the product or the conclusion.

This is where things get even more exciting for marketers as you now get to sell something as though it were your own product, and that in turn means that your business gets the credit. What's more, it means you can change the product to better fit the niche you're in, to be more appealing to your specific audience, or to align with your personal views and ideas.

Another type of product to look into is '**Public Domain Content**'. This is content that gives you all the same rights as PLR content but with one key difference: you don't have to buy it! In order to resell or edit a book or video course that someone else has written, you first need to *buy* the license. That is what you are paying for more than the product itself. But with public domain content, the license belongs to everyone. People are within their rights to sell it to you but you are also within your rights to get it free of charge, as long as you can find it on your own.

Public domain content is simply content that no one owns – and thus everyone owns. It includes content that was published between 1923 and 1963 and which hasn't been renewed or passed on. It also includes content that belonged to authors who have since passed away (though it normally takes 10 years for the content to pass into the public domain).

What this means, is that if you were able to get your hands on a very old manual explaining a subject, then there's no reason you can't edit it slightly and resell it! Just make sure that the content is not too badly out of date.

Finally, if content is under the **creative commons** license, then that means that the individual who created it is happy for you to use it. This might mean you can use it for your own creations but it may not include commercial ventures. Conversely, it might include commercial ventures but require you to give credit to the creator (or potentially to pay them dividends). It might be free for you to use as you wish but not allow you to edit the original.

If something is available only for your own personal use, then that is described as – surprisingly enough – **personal use**. Likewise, you should also consider the term **fair use**. Fair use means that you are using snippets of the original product in order to make a point, or perhaps to review that product. This is more an issue for YouTubers who want to include shots of films they are reviewing; however, this is not something that you will generally need to worry yourself with!

In short, you should be looking for **private label rights** in all cases when considering the products you want to sell!

Chapter 2

Where To Buy Quality Private Label Rights Products

So now you know what PLR means and you know the kinds of rights you need to purchase in order to start profiting.

The next question to ask is where precisely are you going to find those products? Likewise, how do you ensure that the product you are purchasing will be high quality and help you to make sales? How to you avoid a scenario where you end up trying to sell ice to an Inuit?

How to Find High Quality Products

First and foremost, you need to make sure that the products are well written and high quality. The main and most important point is that you need to be providing value to your audience. You can try and 'trick' a buyer into purchasing something that isn't high quality or won't do what they need it to but if you do that, then you'll only end up upsetting your audience, resulting in a scenario where you get lots of returns and where you struggle to sell future books.

And you know what else? People can *tell*.

The problem is that you're not going to know precisely what the book is like until you've bought it but there are a few good ways to avoid buying a dud. First, look at the quality of the website. Is it well written? Is it smartly designed? In all likelihood, the quality of the site is going to be indicative of the quality of the books.

Likewise, see if you can read a snippet from the book. If this isn't immediately available, then consider contacting the seller to ask for a preview. And if that's still not an option, then look for the book's blurb or at least the table of contents.

This isn't just about the writing style either, it's about how interesting and engaging the content is within. If you already have your own list, then of course you need to make sure you are looking for content that fits your niche.

But you also need to ensure that it's genuinely interesting and unique content. Is this content that you would be interested to read? Is it exciting? Does it stand out? Is the title compelling? Does it appear to offer something that other books don't?

Of course, there will always be the temptation to buy books that cover the same old ground. How to get fit, how to build muscle, how to make money online. That's good sure, but if you want to sell in bigger numbers, then you need to sell something with a 'hook' and ideally a specific target audience. People can learn to 'get fit' by reading countless free articles on the web. But if your book is providing some kind of new or unique strategy... well then that's a lot more interesting!

Add to this a great cover design, a bunch of extra features and a generally high production value and you'll have something that will be much easier to sell.

At all costs, avoid poorly written content that has clearly been outsourced overseas, or that has been written with the clear intention of making a 'quick buck'.

In fact, the best thing you can do is to stick predominantly to the established names that sell lots of these products. Better yet, if you should find a product that you really like and that sells well for you, consider returning to that seller in the future!

And what do you know, we've done the hard work for you. Below, you'll find a bunch of different PLR sites where you can rest assured you'll be getting top quality work that you'll be proud to sell!

Some of the Top PLR Sites for Finding Amazing Content to Sell

1. Unstoppable PLR

http://unstoppableplr.com

UnstoppablePLR.com is a site where you can find a large selection of high quality PLR products in a variety of different niches. These include the likes of money making, productivity, lifestyle and health. From living a more minimal lifestyle, to making profit through webinars; you'll find a huge selection of books here, each of which comes with a large selection of extra materials that you can use to sweeten the deal.

Better yet, these products come with all the sales and promotional material you could need to push a large number of units. You get access to a sales page of course, along with images for social media, thank you letters for emails and much more. These are 'done for you' businesses available at great prices and the site comes highly recommended. The site focuses on eBooks though, so if you're looking for courses etc., then you might need to look elsewhere.

2. List Magnets

http://listmagnets.com

List Magnets is another well-regarded site selling PLR content that you can sell for profit. The content covers a range of topics, including business, social media, food, health and more. What's also interesting is that the site offers some free PLR bundles that you can start selling without paying a penny – this is a good way to dip your toes into the water, although of course these products are relatively limited compared with most *paid* content.

The site in general is a little less polished and this follows for the content. The reason for this though, is that the content is aimed more at building a mailing list. These books are meant to be incentives to encourage people to part with their email addresses. As they aren't paying, it's acceptable to make the content a *little* simpler.

3. PLR Sales Funnels

http://plrsalesfunnels.com

You will discover later in this book what a sales funnel is in detail. For now, suffice to say that it is a sequence of marketing that takes someone from being a 'cold lead' to eventually making a purchase. This means you can expect a strong focus on the marketing materials as well as 'freebies' for you to give away to your visitors and maybe eventually slightly less expensive items.

All of this will help to 'warm up' your customers before getting them to make a purchase. It's also a very good way to build trust and authority over time before eventually making a sale.

The site is well designed and the content is great quality. The only limitation is that once again, the focus is strongly on digital products and in this case, it is almost entirely marketing based.

(It's kind of a head trip when you think about it: this is someone that is trying to make money online by selling products about making money online, to other people that want to make money online by selling books about making money online, to people who just want to make money online...)

4. HQ PLR Store

http://hqplrstore.com

This is another great source of PLR content, all with lots of extra materials for helping you to sell onward. These are complete 'biz in a box' products, which once again means you should be getting *everything* you need from which to start profiting from an online business selling products. Again, this largely focuses on the 'make money online' niche and once again, the quality is high and reliable.

There are some interesting topics here that you don't tend to see so often too, such as 'WhatsApp Marketing'!

5. Internet Slayers

https://internetslayers.com/

Internet Slayers is one of the less high-quality looking sites but in this case, first impressions may be a little deceiving. The site is not the most polished but the content is very well written with professional looking imagery and lots of extras. Some of these products come with 200+ items thrown in, which is excellent value for money for you *and* for your customers.

What's more, is that the content is written by someone who clearly cares about quality. Either way, this is good stuff and another benefit is that the content is not in the make money niche for a change – rather it is focused on health with topics on nutrition, diet, exercise, yoga and more.

Also interesting to note is that you can buy smaller packages and items here. You don't just have to buy full products – you can also get packs of articles to use on a website (remember they won't be unique content though) or to send as emails.

6. Content Shortcuts

http://contentshortcuts.com

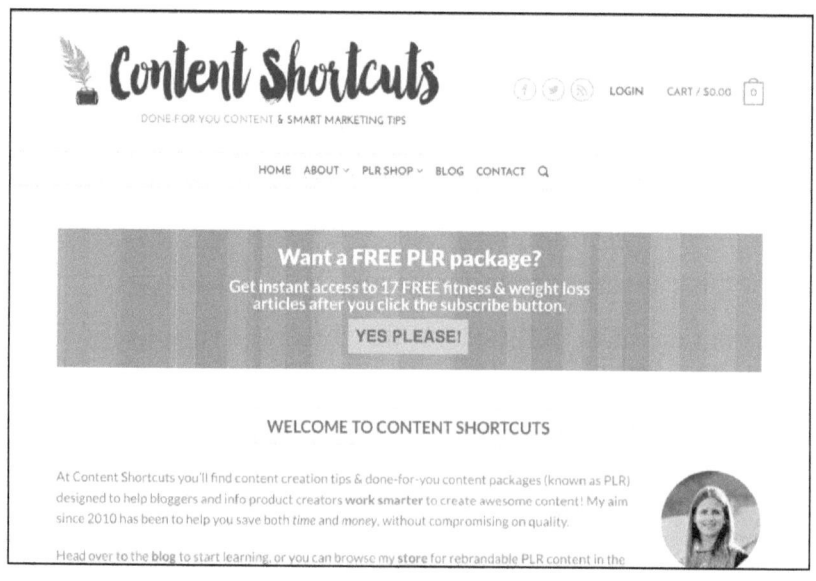

Content Shortcuts is somewhat similar to Internet Slayers and provides lots of PLR content. They cover a range of topics, including health and fitness, as well as productivity, making money online and more. They are well priced and if you sign up to the mailing list, you can get one PLR package for free.

7. PLR Mini Mart

http://plrminimart.com

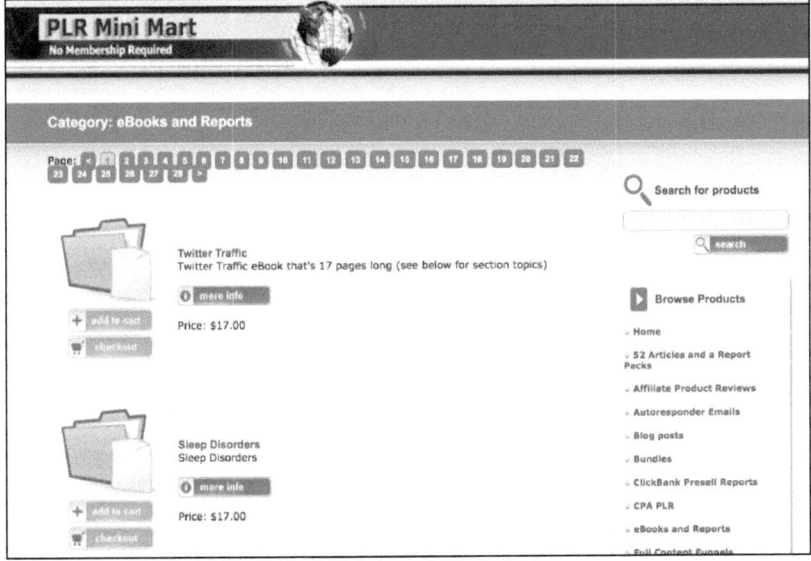

PLR Mini Mart is a store that was launched in 2006 and continues to have new content added to it regularly. The author of the products is Tiffany Lambert, who wrote for a myriad of top marketers such as John Reese. Content is sold in the form of eBooks, product reviews, articles, reports, and more – with topics spanning across many different niches.

Content can be purchased in small doses (such as one pack of five articles) or as full content funnels, giving you everything you need for a site – such as the opt in report, blog post articles, product reviews, an info product to sell, email autoresponders and more.

You can also buy by the pack or get a lifetime (total) membership, which gives you access to all current PLR as well as anything added to the store in the future.

8. PLRXtreme

http://plrxtreme.com/monthly

PLRXtreme is owned by PLR veteran, Edmund Loh.

PLRXtreme have been providing high quality Internet marketing courses since 2005.

You'll find eBooks, videos courses, and more. The products are packaged into modules, and you'll find each package includes all the modules you need to customize the product.

And Then There's Many More...

This is only a small selection of the many different places where you can find PLR content. To find many more, just do a quick Google for 'PLR Products' and remember to use the checks that we recommended above.

Save Money with our Exclusive PLR Memberships

Our memberships allow you to **maximize your marketing** with content by providing you fresh content, month after month. Keep your readers informed, grow your search engine traffic and become a trusted resource with one of the following.

Our marketing PLR membership comes with articles, reports, slide shows, images and more. Or if you're a PLR seller, you can sign up for our resell membership.

Click the links below to get more information on each membership:

Self-Improvement Content Membership

Our Self-Improvement Mini Membership is where you can get personal empowerment and self growth content to feed your readers and exercise their minds. Click here to secure your spot.

Health Content Membership

From prevention to health care, you can get a nice burst of health content at a pretty amazing price...each and every month. Click here to secure your spot.

Marketing Content Membership

All kinds of topics of interest to the business-to-business market. Everything from starting a business, marketing and more. Click here for details.

Resell Rights PLR Membership

If you've always wanted to start your own PLR business or are on the lookout for more PLR you can sell, here's your chance. We include content on a variety of topics each month that you can sell as PLR. Click here to sell PLR.

All our monthly memberships are backed by our **full 30-day satisfaction money-back guarantee**, so you can try them with confidence.

Search for PLR

How to Make PLR Work for You

PLR is a tremendous time saver, but it's just one important piece of the content marketing puzzle. When you buy PLR, you still have to publish the content, connect with your audience and grow your sales...and that doesn't just happen all on its own.

Recently, we've had more customers come to ask and ask us to help them so they can **use PLR to the fullest**. Some people need help with nuts and bolts type stuff, while others are looking for more advanced help with marketing.

Well to satisfy all these needs, we will be releasing a **complete course** to help you work through publishing your content, monetizing it, growing your list and expanding your traffic.

Click here to get started.

One example of a good one is All Private Label Content (http://allprivatelabelcontent.com), another is Easy PLR (http://www.easyplr.com/) which covers a good range of topics including things like tech and anxiety; but there are many more.

You can also find other good resources this way. For instance, http://dfytemplates.com is a good place to find templates for sales pages and other materials for helping you to sell. This can help fill in the blanks if you find a PLR product but not the marketing materials to go with it!

Chapter 3

Start With The Right Tools

If you want to be successful with PLR, then it can be a good idea to invest a little in your business. One of the best ways you can do that is by investing in your hardware and software. By upgrading your capabilities, you will improve your ability to make your own edits to improve upon the original products or just to make them a little better suited to your specific branding (whatever that may be!).

So, what kind of tools can you make use of as a PLR reseller? Here are some of the most useful…

Image Editing and Word Processing

Perhaps the most basic place to start is with word processing software. If you are going to make edits to the actual content rather than just the cover, then you will need a piece of software that allows you to open and edit the documents that your content is made up of.

Most of your PLR products will come in .doc or .docx format. This is of course the Microsoft Word format and thus downloading MS Office could be a good place to start. With that said though, you could find you are able to use other products, such as Open Office or Google Docs.

While MS Office is particularly feature-rich and very much an industry standard tool, it unfortunately also costs a recurring monthly fee. Open Office does essentially the same things but is free. You might find a couple of compatibility issues but on the whole, it should be smooth sailing.

Another free option is Google Docs. Google Docs is a cloud service that began life as Google Drive – a cloud storage solution – but grew to include its own tools such as a spreadsheet tool (Google Sheets), Word Processor (Google Docs) and more. This is excellent for collaboration, as it allows you to make changes that will instantly be available to anyone else with access to the

Google Drive folder. Moreover, you can make comments and annotations for others to see.

This is less convenient for editing PLR content, however, as you'll probably have the document on your computer, and you'll likely find this brings up even more compatibility issues than something like Open Office.

This is not a bad solution but if you plan on doing this a lot, then MS Word is a worthwhile investment. MS Word will allow you to create headings and titles and to autogenerate a table of contents from this. It will also let you do other impressive things, such as adding watermarks or page numbers. While other tools might do the same, they will possibly go about it in a different way to the original creator, thereby creating more work for you!

As for redesigning your covers or creating images for inside the book, this will probably benefit from Photoshop. Most of the covers that you get with your PLR content will also be available in editable Photoshop file format. This will allow you to do things like editing individual layers: for instance, you can alter text that is hovering on top of a background image, or you can alter just the background image and leave the text as it is.

The only problem with this, is that Photoshop is actually a rather expensive product. In order to gain access to it, you will need to sign up for the Adobe Creative Cloud and you can choose to give yourself access to the full suite of apps that come with that, or just the few tools that you actually need (though this will limit you to two).

There is a free one-month trial that you can use. This will allow you to edit the cover of one PLR cover, but of course that's not going to be especially convenient if you want to do this on a regular basis and you have lots of books you need to edit!

An alternative is once again to use free software. A good example of this is GIMP, which can do nearly everything that Photoshop can do and is completely free of charge. Again, the issue here is compatibility and there is no guarantee that GIMP will be able to work with all of the files you get – this will depend on how the creator decided to work!

That said, if you only have access to a PNG or a JPG, you can still do a lot with GIMP or Photoshop. You'll still be able to airbrush, or to apply effects and filters. And if the book designer has been smart, then they will have placed the title against a plain colored background which you can edit without needing to work with layers.

Again, this is all at the discretion of the creator and something you need to consider when choosing which PLR product is right for you.

However, if you want to make logos or images, then there might be a little more reason to invest in the Creative Cloud and that is so that you can get Illustrator. Illustrator is the software that is considered the industry standard for making logos and other professional designs. The reason for this is that it creates 'vector files'. Vector files are files that allow you to move, bend and delete the individual lines that make up your image – as well as to resize them. That means they can be resized endlessly with no loss of quality which means that once more, they can be edited in a way that appears seamless.

It is down to you to decide how much editing you want to do and what kinds of books you'll be reselling!

Web Services

You can choose to skip that last chapter if you so wish: there is no requirement for you to make any edits and if you prefer, you can sell your product just as it is!

But what you will definitely need to do, no matter what business model you choose to pursue, is to set up a website/page from which you can start selling your product. You might already have this, in which case some of these suggestions won't be relevant. But for everyone else, the following will be absolutely required...

Web Hosting

Web hosting means somewhere for you to store the files that make up your website online.

We recommend HostGator (www.hostgator.com) or CoolHandle (www.coolhandle.com), both of which will provide a lot of extra features and benefits on top of basic hosting – including a range of tools to help you manage emails, upload and download files, edit files on the fly, improve your security or even install WordPress with a single click.

You can purchase one of the more basic packages, as this will give you enough space to store the files you need as well as enough bandwidth to handle the volume of traffic (unless your product turns out to be the next Pokemon Go, in which case you can always go ahead and upgrade your account.

As well as the space to store your files, you'll also need a domain name, which of course is the address that people will type into their URL bar when they want to find you. You can get this through your hosting provider, or through NameCheap (www.namecheap.com) or GoDaddy (www.godaddy.com).

Finally, to help with transferring files, an FTP software like FileZilla (https://filezilla-project.org) can be a very useful tool indeed. This will allow you to upload files to your hosting account without having to do so through your browser. It's also handy for making backups or fixing issues when things go wrong with your WordPress files.

Building Your Sales Page

You'll also want a payment processor, which will allow you to create your own 'buy now' button. This is important – if you don't replace the buy now button, then you may just be making money for the person that sold you the product! This will be tied to your own account and that way, you can withdraw the cash into your own bank. PayPal (www.paypal.com) or Stripe (www.stripe.com) are good choices.

Depending on the type of package you have purchased, you might find that your product comes with ready-made files to run the website. In this case, you can simply swap out the 'Buy Now' button and any of the text that you want to change and then just upload all the files to your domain.

On the other hand, you might just have been given the text and in that case, you will need to create the actual HTML page that this text is going to go on.

To do this, you might want to install WordPress, which you can do through your hosting provider or through WordPress.com (www.wordpress.com). From here, you may wish to install a theme like OptimizePress (www.optimizepress.com), which will automatically transform your site into the perfect size and shape to be a sales page! You can also use something like Infusionsoft, (www.infusionsoft.com), which combines an autoresponder with a sales page and a 'buy now' button all in one!

You can also sell through a Project Management System such as JVZoo (www.jvzoo.com) or ClickBank (www.clickbank.com). By the way, these also happen to be affiliate marketing networks, meaning that you can use them in order to sell products via affiliates. An affiliate is of course a marketer that will get commission whenever they sell your product. This means you can have more people helping to drive traffic to your PLR product so that you don't even need to do the marketing legwork! We'll talk more about this later…

Autoresponder

Finally, you might want an autoresponder. This is a piece of software that you use to build mailing lists. This allows you to collect the emails of people who think they might be interested in buying your products and then to send them messages to encourage them to come back and buy. It lets you build trust and it lets you establish yourself as an authority.

The purpose of the autoresponder is to allow you to keep all your contacts managed in one place and to handle things such as new subscribers or people choosing to leave the list without you having to do everything manually. Good options include GetResponse (www.getresponse.com), AWeber (www.aweber.com) and MailChimp (www.mailchimp.com).

Chapter 4

How To Customize a PLR Product

Selling PLR content is one of the easiest and most effective ways to start making money online.

However, it is also true to say that there is no such thing as a completely 'perfect' business model. The biggest limitation here is that you will be going up against a lot of competition. You are not only competing with other sellers in the same niche, you are competing with other sellers that have the *exact* same product as you do!

This can also create problems if someone buys your product and then realizes that they have already bought it elsewhere.

Likewise, you will want to do a *little* work, just to make your product look like something you would sell. You want to put your brand on it and your name so that your audience feels that you created it. This is important because it means that your product will not only make you money but also further build the brand loyalty that you need to start making big sales through return customers.

With so many people buying the same PLR products, how do you separate yourself and make sure it doesn't seem like you're selling the same thing?

Avoiding Direct Competition

One thing to keep in mind here, is that you can actually sell your product relatively easily without worrying about others finding it. It's normal to worry that someone is going to stumble upon your product under a different name and you'll be rumbled, but the reality is that the Internet is a *very* big place. That is to say, most people will never even come into contact with the other sellers.

This is especially true if you are selling to your own established audience.

But one way you can make extra sure of this is to find a different way to position your book and a way to make it appeal to a slightly different audience.

Surprisingly, changing the title of a book can make a huge difference to the way that the content within is interpreted while still keeping it relevant.

For example, let's say you have a book titled *'Kitsch Wedding – How to Have the Cutesy, Retro-Themed Wedding of Your Dreams'*. This will appeal to a slightly different audience than *'Trendy Wedding – How to Throw a Modern, Trendy Wedding in Keeping with Today's Style'*.

The thing is, today's style *is* quite kitsch, but what you've done here is to make the book sound like two different things while still keeping the content that follows relevant.

Likewise, you could turn *'Eating Right: The Easy Diet That Anyone Can Stick To'*, into *'Diet Explained for Student Dietitians'*. The target audience here is completely different for the two books but the topic is the same.

If you're willing to go a little further and actually edit the content that you're selling, then you can be more 'on the nose'. You could turn *'Diet Advice for Students'* into *'Diet Advice for Young Athletes'*. You'll need to change some of the wording but that is all – and you completely eliminate the likelihood of people stumbling upon the same content.

BUT, in order to do this, you *must read the content*! Hopefully you're a fast reader…

More Ways to Customize an eBook

Other things you can do to make the ebook uniquely your own include...

o Give the product a new title/name

o Redesign the cover

o Reword the content with your voice/writing style

o Read out the content and record it to sell as an audio book, for a YouTube series or for a podcast!

o Add extra content making it more meaty or strip down content to make it to-the-point

o Dissect/extract some content to use as blog posts or for your email autoresponder series

o Add extra content from other sources and/or write a foreword

o Purchase multiple different eBooks and then combine them into one 'uber' eBook

o Purchase multiple different eBooks and mix and match the chapters (this is something to consider when choosing which eBook to buy – a smartly designed PLR product might well use a more modular construction to allow for this sort of thing)

- o Add additional images

- o Alter the formatting to give a unique style

- o Use the content inside your membership site

- o Use the eBook to promote other products that you want to sell – even consider adding affiliate links!

Chapter 5

How To Get Your PLR Product Redesigned and Rewritten

Unfortunately, not everyone has the skills or the know-how they need in order to rework a digital product. Maybe you want to reword the book but don't have any particular writing skills?

Perhaps you'd like to change the cover but you don't have access to image editing software or any particular artistic eye?

In those cases then, your best option is to outsource the process of improving the book to someone who *does* have the skills.

There are a few ways to do this.

Finding Designers

One option is to use Fiverr (www.fiverr.com). Fiverr is a website where you can find a huge range of different services (and products), all sold for – you guessed it - $5.

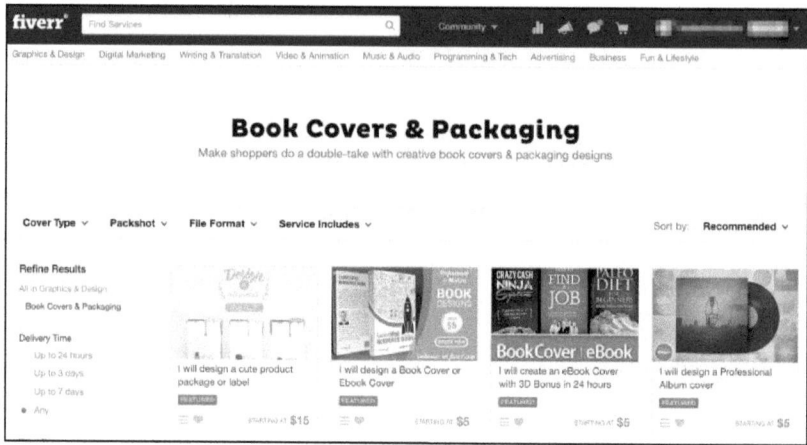

In many cases, these can be 'upgraded' to bigger jobs. For example, an artist that offers to make logos for $5 might offer to redesign a book cover for $20. That said though, you can normally find skilled individuals that are willing to redesign a book cover for $5!

There are also other places to look for image designs. One good option is to go to a marketing forum such as Warrior Forum (www.warriorforum.com). More specifically, look inside its 'Warriors For Hire' section (http://www.warriorforum.com/warriors- hire/).

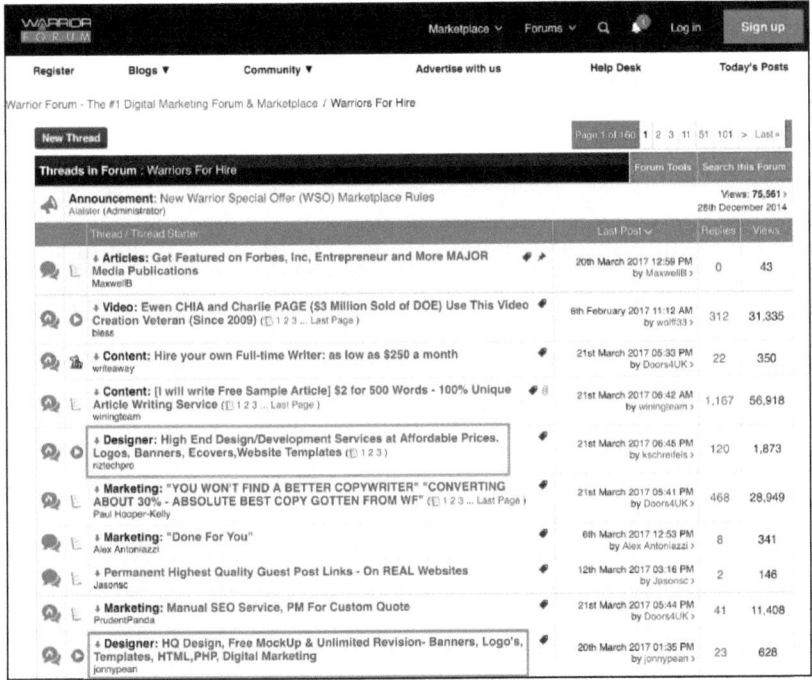

Here, you'll be able to meet and work with other people who are in the same business as you: trying to make money online. This will include SEO providers (search engine optimizers), web designers and other PLR resellers! It also includes graphics designers and a good way to get a great design for a low price is to run a 'contest'. Here, you invite the members to submit their best designs and offer to pay a price for your favorite one. This works well for you because it gives you lots of designs to choose from and you only need to pay for the one you like best.

A great site that revolves around this concept entirely is 99Designs (www.99designs.com). This site is a 'crowdsourcing' site for getting professional designs and the best compliment is that it has been used successfully to create covers for even *New York Times* bestsellers. One such example is author of the *Four Hour Workweek*, Tim Ferriss.

Finding Writers

If you want to find someone to rewrite some of your content, however, then you will likely need to find a writer and as this is a considerably bigger job, and you may want to look outside of Fiverr. One good alternative is to look to one of the many 'freelancing websites'.

These include the likes of Freelancer.com (www.freelancer.com) and UpWork (www.upwork.com). Here, you can find trained writers who will likely charge 'per word' for making edits to your books.

They can also be hired for a range of other tasks too, whether you want someone to write you a new sales page or a new set of email marketing messages!

Likewise, you can also find this kind of work over at Warrior Forum. Either look for people advertising their skills, or post your own thread announcing the work and inviting those willing to help to get in touch.

Chapter 6

How To Get Your Sales Page Up And Running

The sales page is one of the single most important aspects of your PLR business.

A sales page, as the name implies, is the page from which you will sell your product. What makes this different from something like an ecommerce store however, is that it is only going to be focused on selling the *one* product.

Why Sales Pages Are Designed the Way They Are

And in fact, that is *all* that it is going to be focused on. Your traditional sales page is going to have a very distinctive design.

Normally, this will be laid out as one very long, tall and narrow page. This page will have no external links and no 'chrome' – that means no navigational links either. You're not going to find links here to the homepage, nor will you find links to other products, a blog, or anything of the sort.

That's because any link like this is going to be a distraction. You want to give your visitors only two ways of getting away: clicking 'buy' or clicking 'back'.

The job of the sales page is to make sure that they choose the former and the way it does that, is by immediately grabbing attention with bold statements and then encouraging the reader to keep on scrolling.

This is where the long, narrow layout comes in. The fact that your page is tall, means that each paragraph will lead very quickly down to the next line and force the reader to keep scrolling. This has a somewhat hypnotic effect on the reader: as they scroll, they feel more and more 'committed' to the post.

They are taking steps further and further into your world and eventually, they'll feel like they really want to buy to prevent the time spent reading from being a waste!

How to Write Stellar Sales Copy

If the seller of the PLR product you're reselling was smart, then they will have written their sales copy in such a way as to really encourage this continuous reading. To do that, they will have probably started with a *narrative structure*.

I read a quote somewhere that 'storytelling is SEO for the human brain'. This is *very* true and in fact, you'll find that it's very hard to stop reading when someone is spinning a good yarn. We have been telling and listening to stories since we first came down from the trees and as such, we are very much evolved to want to hear how a story will end.

Another benefit of a story is that it makes you more relatable, it makes the story more relatable and it make what you have to say inherently more interesting as a result.

A 'story' could begin with something about you: 'I used to be overweight' or 'I used to be unhappy with my career', or it could be something about the product, 'It was only an amazing researcher who made a discovery that would change the way we approach fitness...'.

Some other strategies can similarly help to encourage engagement, retention and conversion.

One example of this is to ask rhetorical questions: 'Would you like to be better looking? More confident?' Doing this works because it is asking us to think and when we think, we engage. No longer is the reader a passive consumer of your content, they are now actively taking part in a back and forth and thus they are less likely to just leave without taking anything in.

Most important of all though is to focus on your *value proposition* - which comes from understanding the product that you are trying to sell. A value proposition is simply the way in which a product is going to offer value to the customer. The old saying goes that you 'don't sell hats, you sell warm heads'. What this means is that the thing you're selling is more than the sum of its parts. What's most important is the way that it creates tangible benefit for the buyer. The way that it makes them *feel*.

So, when you sell someone a book on how to lose weight, complete with a diet guide, a mind map, training videos and more, you have two options:

1) Focus on how much value you are offering by illustrating how many different things are included for this 'low, low price'

2) Focus on how the buyer is going to feel, how they will fit into smaller clothes, how they will attract the attention of the opposite sex

The second option is *by far* the more strategic way to sell and the more effective because it speaks to universal truths.

Another goal of a good sales page is to build trust and authority. You want to make sure that the person buying from you believes that you know what you're talking about and you want them to feel secure making the purchase.

This is one reason you should use a tool like PayPal to process orders – it creates familiarity and trust because it's something people have used before or have at least heard of.

Another way to build trust is to encourage people to believe your claims and assertions. One way to do this is to try and back up what you say with figures, studies and authority sources. Don't just claim that a certain type of diet can help people lose weight: show them the numbers!

Finally, once you've piqued the interest and built the trust, the final goal of good sales copy is to make someone click to buy. To do this, you need to create a sense of urgency. People tend to make purchase decisions based on their emotions, not their logic. If you give your buyers time to consider whether or not they really need something, then they will normally come to the conclusion that they do not.

But promoting that value proposition has made the product seem life changing. So too has focusing on the way it makes them *feel*. You now have them strongly considering impulsively clicking 'Buy' and you need to make sure that they go ahead and do it.

To do that, you can invent a limited supply. Another option is to introduce a special offer that will only last a certain amount of time. Now, the user has to act fast or risk not getting the product or paying more for it. This can be enough to encourage them to quickly click the buy button, rather than having time to reconsider!

Making Edits and Adding a PayPal Button

Most of this will already be done for you. This is something that PLR creators know inside out and do for a living, so you can rest assured that your sales page will be tested and re-tested to ensure that it drives conversions. Using the information above, you can simply make any changes that you feel are pertinent in order to lean on your buyers a little more. This is especially useful if you understand your specific audience, and that way, you can think about what *they* want and how you're going to offer it.

One of the simplest ways to look at selling any product is simply as solving problems. Identify a specific problem that a specific group has and then solve it. That way, you can almost guarantee a steady flow of sales!

What you also need to change, however, is your payment button. To do this, you're going to use PayPal to create your own 'Buy Now' button (called the action button to use industry parlance).

First, you'll need to create your own PayPal Business or PayPal Premier Account. If you haven't already done that, then you'll find instructions on PayPal's own website.

From there, you then need to build the payment button. This should allow people to pay through their own PayPal account, or using a credit or debit card if they don't yet have an account.

To go ahead, log in to your PayPal account and then find the 'Tools' option at the top of the page and then 'All Tools'. Here, you should find the 'PayPal Buttons' option and you'll be able to click 'Open'.

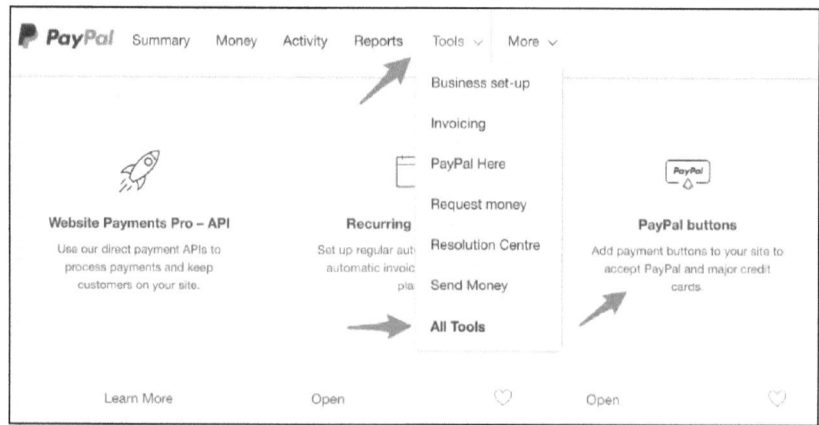

On the '**My Saved Buttons**' page, you'll see a heading called 'Related Items' and under this, you'll see the option to 'Create New Button'.

When you click that, the '**Create PayPal Button**' page will open.

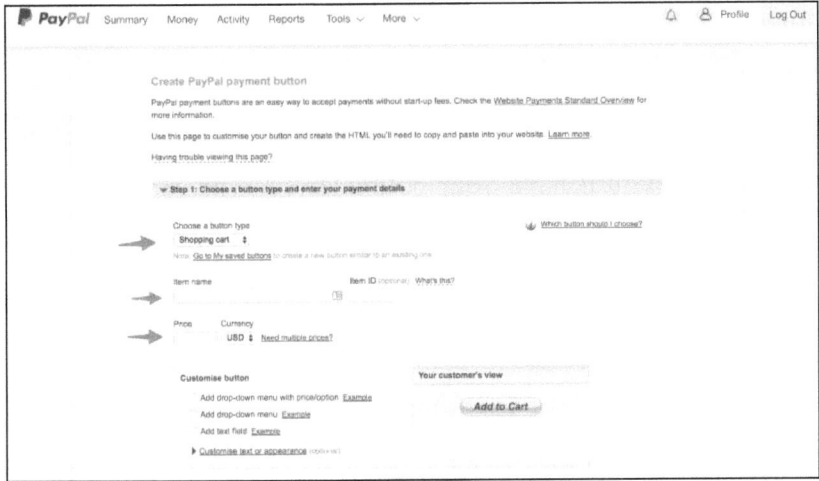

You'll then be presented with a drop-down menu, from which you can select the type of PayPal button you want to implement. For example, you might want to create an 'Add to Basket' option, which is great for ecommerce. For our purposes though, you're almost always going to want to use the 'Buy Now' button.

Next, you'll need to add an **Item Name**. This of course will be the name of the digital product you're selling! If you use tracking numbers for your own tracking purposes, then this is the opportunity to add that too. But it is entirely optional.

Under price, you're of course going to want to add your chosen price for the product. You might want to add multiple pricing options, in which case you'll see options for that too. You can also change the default currency.

Once you're happy with everything, just click on '**Create Button**' and you'll have your button saved. This will generate HTML code and from there, you can copy and paste the code to your web page.

Note that you may also want to customize the appearance of your button. Click '**Customize Text or Appearance**' and then choose from the options that follow. This includes the option to make the button smaller, to show credit card logos or even to set a custom background image for the button.

You'll also have the option to choose which page your buyer gets sent to following their purchase. This might be where they can download their product, or it might just be a thank you page (you can send out the product yourself in that case, or you can set up some kind of auto-generated email to do the same).

Think about how you want the experience to be for your buyers, and if you've been given a 'thank you page', then of course use that!

Side note: If you would like an alternate method of adding an order button with the added features of managing your product, consider using JVZoo (http://jvzoo.com).

You can view the following tutorial on how to setup a sales funnel in JVZoo:

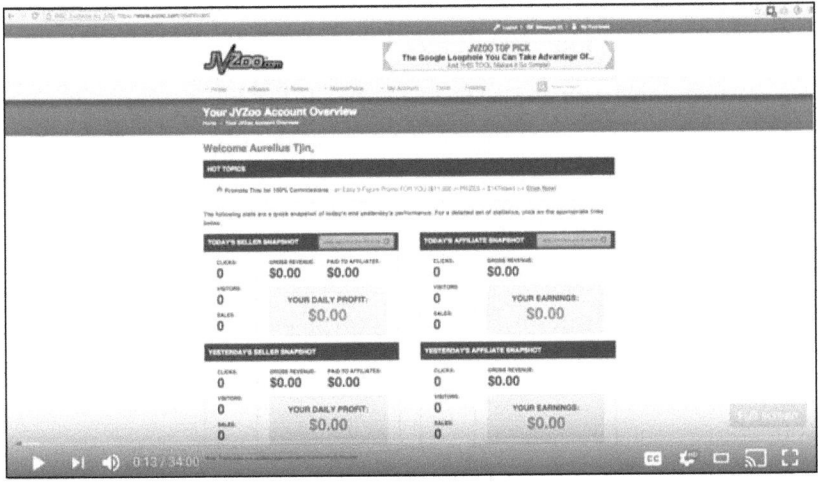

https://www.youtube.com/watch?v=p-jO4l0QniY

Uploading Your Files

Once you've made the changes you want, you should find it's relatively simple to upload your files and get going. If you're using your own WordPress site, then you can simply copy and paste the text and upload the images through the control panel.

Otherwise, if you have ready-to-go HTML files, you'll want to use either the file manager that came with your hosting provider, or FileZilla. The objective is then to upload the files to the root directory of your website. Look for the folder with the name of your website and the primary domain will be rooted in the public_html folder. The file called 'Index.html' is the one that visitors will see first.

To do this through Filezilla, you'll need to enter the URL (with the prefix FTP) and then your username and password to connect.

From there, you can drag and drop the files as you would do in explorer and they will begin to copy over.

To do it through the file manager that came with your hosting account, simply find the manager in cPanel (this is the control panel that comes with most larger hosting accounts) and then locate the 'Upload' button. From here, you'll be able to select the files you want and then watch as they are uploaded one at a time. Again though, just make sure you're in the right directory first!

Important: Before you 'go live' and start promoting your sales page, *always* make sure that you test the page and also test the button. Otherwise, you might find that the page doesn't show, that the payment doesn't come through to you or that your customers are unable to access their products. The latter can hurt your reputation and prevent future sales.

So, go through the entire process using a friend's computer or another account and see how they would experience it. You can always then just refund the sale in order to get the PayPal fee returned to you!

Chapter 7

How To Get Your Opt-In Page Up

Another important aspect of most PLR packages is the 'opt-in' page. This works similarly to a sales page in that it has a singular purpose, but it is different in that the purpose in question is unique from the sales page.

The idea of an opt-in page is to allow you to build a mailing list filled with leads that will potentially want to buy from you.

Here's the deal: trying to get someone who has just landed on your website to buy a product from you immediately is a fool's errand. All that will tend to happen is that they will feel frustrated at being 'sold to' and then leave'.

But with an opt-in page – the chance to sign up to an email list – you are offering *free information* instead. This is much easier to convince a stranger to go for and you can think of it a little like introducing yourself to a hot date before asking for their phone number. Most PLR packages will give you an opt-in page and will then also provide you with an autoresponder sequence (remember the autoresponder manages your email marketing) that will consist of several emails that have been designed to encourage people to open them and then to build trust and authority so that they become interested in buying from you.

What most PLR packages will *also* provide though – and this is even more important – is some kind of incentive. The incentive is the free item that your visitors will want badly enough in order to be willing to hand over their account details.

If you've ever seen the (highly annoying) videos from Tai Lopez on YouTube, then this is a good demonstration of how a sales funnel works. Tai starts by bombarding cold leads with videos through YouTube advertising. Most of us click 'Skip' but a few will be won over by his promise to 'change your life in 3 minutes'.

Of course one of the '3 amazing tips' that Tai offers needs further elaboration but *don't worry* – the information he is offering is completely free of charge and you can find it by clicking the link below. So, you do that and you're taken to his page. Indeed that information *is* free but in order to get it, you need to fill out your email to get it sent to you (this is to 'prevent spam' or some nonsense of course). So, you do that and you get your free report.

In the free report, the true product is promoted for $100. (The $100 product also promotes a $1,000 product FYI).

And if you aren't won over by this, then the several emails that follow will be enough to encourage you to reconsider making a purchase.

You've gone from someone who is annoyed by Tai and wants to be left alone, to someone who just spent $1,000 to visit his seminar. This is the power of a 'sales funnel' and the first and most important step in that is to promote a mailing list via an incentive – or a 'magnet' (hence the name of the site ListMagnets).

How to Set Up Your Opt-In Page

To get your opt-in page online, you can simply follow the same steps we used to get the sales page up and running. The difference though is that instead of setting up a 'Buy Now' button, your job is instead to set up a subscribe button.

And to do that, you will need to use your autoresponder. We looked at three earlier on but the one that I most recommend is AWeber. To use this to create your list, click the button along the top that says 'Manage Lists' and then select 'Create A List'.

From here, you will then create your list. This is one great thing about AWeber – it allows you to have multiple lists at once so that you can have one for each digital product if you so wish and/or one for your overarching brand.

You'll need to enter some details such as a contact address and your website and then the information that you want to be displayed about you when the emails go out. You can also name your list and you should choose something logical here in the interest of organization.

Describe the list and then make a message for your confirmation. Most autoresponders now default to a 'double opt-in', which means that your new visitors will need to sign up and *then* confirm their address. This is an important way to prevent people from confirming by accident, to prevent people from signing up who never check their emails, and to prevent spam. Building a big list is not important – building a highly targeted and engaged list is what matters!

It's up to you what your welcome message looks like but of course you want to make sure that it includes a link to the product that your subscribers have been promised! You can also pick your own subject heading but it's a good idea to choose from one of the 'pre-approved' messages as these will improve click through rates while also avoiding spam filters.

Click 'Approve Message & Create List' and your list is now ready to go!

Next is to make the form that will go on your website. To do this, you need to select the 'Sign Up Forms' tab from the menu and then choose 'Create a Sign Up Form'. The steps that follow are very self-explanatory and easy to follow. You can choose which template you want to use if any or you can create something new. Choose something that will match the design of your site while also standing out.

You'll also need to choose what information you want to collect. The simpler you keep this, the easier it will be to convince people to sign up. But with that said, more data will make it easier for you to sell and will even mean that your mailing list itself might be worth something in the future, thus meaning that you can actually sell it!

Choose the header to decide how you want the form to announce itself and pick a name for it. You also want to choose a thank you page, which is another place where you can include your download link if you prefer. This might be predetermined by the files that you have been provided with… go with it!

And *of course*, you need to test that this all works again before going live!

Chapter 8

How To Start Making Sales

Now everything is up and running, the next step is to start making sales of your products. With the sales page up and running and presuming that it has been well-designed, making sales *should* be as simple as just driving traffic to your site. That said though, you also need to make sure that you're driving the right kind of targeted traffic (i.e., people who might actually want to buy from you) and you need to reach those people somehow. The tips in this chapter will fill you in…

Facebook Ads

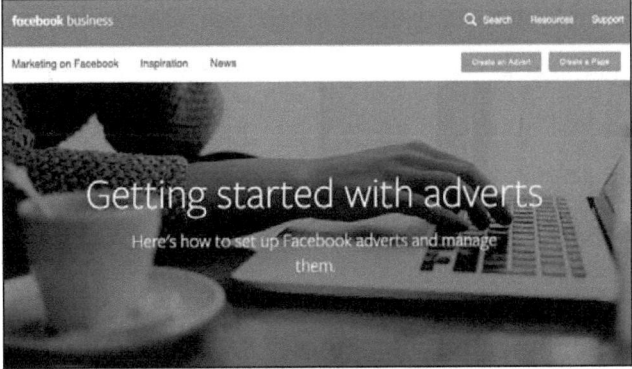

One of the easiest ways to start generating sales for your product is to promote your sales page via Facebook Ads. These are PPC ads, meaning they are 'pay per click' – you only pay when someone actually clicks one! Better yet, they are highly targeted, allowing you to filter who you display the ads to; based on the copious amounts of information that they have provided the social network with. You can show your ads to people in certain regions, people of a certain age, or people with particular interests. You can choose their relationship status, their income, whether they're a homeowner…

And this is incredibly useful, because if you promote your book on wedding planning to someone you know is engaged, then your chances of being successful are high. If your book is 'wedding planning on a budget' and you target engaged people with a smaller target income, then your chances of success are even higher!

Because you know how much you are paying per click, that means you know precisely how much you are paying for each visitor. If you also know what percentage of your visitors buy your products and you know how much profit you make from each of those sales, then you can combine all that knowledge in order to calculate the amount you can pay for your clicks and still keep making profit.

Remember, the key is not to get as many clicks as you can as this will *cost* you money. The key is to get clicks from people who know what they're clicking – so be highly descriptive in your ads!

That way, you'll get a higher conversion rate and higher profit margin.

Announce on Social Media/Blog/Email

A lot of people reading this book will already be running a website successfully. In that case, they might be reading with the hopes of increasing their profits from said website or blog by selling a product, rather than relying purely on clicks in order to generate income.

If that's you, then hopefully you will already have some kind of following on social media, you'll already have people reading your blog and you'll already have a mailing list. The simple way to start making sales then is to simply shout about the new product through these channels and make it sound amazing. If you've done your work, then the followers should be fans of yours that trust what you have to say and what you have to sell and this will mean big conversions for you – it all comes down to how well you treat your followers.

Either way, you can use this strategy to get a big boost in sales early on and especially if you are smart about building hype. Don't just announce your product and hope people start buying it: instead, let interest build slowly and get feedback. Tell your audience you're working on something awesome and let them know roughly when it will launch. If you tell them about it before they can own it, it will seem considerably more desirable. We always want what we can't have!

Purchase Solo Ads

If you don't have your own audience though, then you can always use someone else's! This is the idea behind solo ads: they allow you to buy the right to send a sponsored message to someone else's mailing list. For a small fee then, you can have a big blogger promote your product and mention that you're selling it. You can buy these from sites like clickonomy.com (www.clickonomy.com), clickdrop.com (www.clickdrop.com) and UDIMI (www.udimi.com). Just make sure that the list you're paying to advertise on is large, well suited to your specific niche and the product you're selling is high quality. You want to choose a list that is normally filled with excellent, high quality information as this way, the subscribers will be accustomed to actually wanting to *read* the messages that come through, meaning that they'll be far more likely to actually read the advert that you paid for!

If you don't go the solo ads route, another option is to do an 'Ad Swap'. This means that you post to your mailing list in exchange for someone else posting to theirs – creating a mutually beneficial exchange.

Finally, consider looking into other forms of influencer marketing. This might mean asking a prominent YouTuber or Twitter user to mention your product. You can supply them with a free copy to review, or you can pay for the service.

Chapter 9

How To Increase Sales Using Upsells

Simply trying to sell as much of your product as possible is a relatively modest aim though. Better yet, is to use your new product in order to sell *other* new products. This way, you can scale your business and you can grow your profits.

An upsell simply means that you use one sale in order to make another sale. Normally, the second sale will be bigger and more expensive, or it might just be a matter of expanding the product that you're selling into a bigger package.

For example then, if your PLR package came with a lot of free materials (mind map, cheat sheet etc.), then you could hold some of them back and keep the price a little lower. Then, when the buyer is at the POS (Point Of Sale – the moment before they click 'buy'), you then advertise that they can expand their package to the 'premium package' for just $15 more.

This can encourage people to spend more than they otherwise would. The reason for this is that they will now be poised to buy and they've already made the difficult decision to spend money. They've even entered their details, so the 'barrier to sale' is incredible small. What's more, is that they're already spending $50, in which case, $15 is not much extra at all.

And no one likes knowing that they are missing out or getting the 'dud' version.

And this holds true even for those customers that never would have agreed to a $65 product up front!

There are other ways you can sweeten the deal too. How about recording a video/audio version of your main product? This is an excellent way to boost the value of your product and to earn much more as a result.

Another option is simply to bundle multiple books together into a big package – ensuring that those books are relevant. The good thing here is that it costs you nothing to provide what will seem like *twice* the value that you were providing before.

Making Extra Sales

You can also use your initial sale to make completely separate, unrelated sales. One way to do this is to sell a 'bigger ticket' item, which is one of the main reasons to build a sales funnel in the first place.

If you happen to have access to an amazing product that you think you could sell for $700, then you need to be very careful about how you're going to promote that product. The best way to go ahead is to encourage your customer to make a $35 purchase first.

Why?

Because this way, they will have seen that you are capable of providing value and that you can be trusted. Moreover, they'll know precisely how to order from you and their details might even still be saved on your site! It's simplicity itself for them to just turn that small order into a big one, so you just need *one moment* where their desire outstrips their 'sensible' brain.

As well as promoting this bigger product through emails, you can also include references to it *within* the main product you're selling.

Another option is to offer a money off bonus to those who have bought from you. They now not only have that trust, familiarity and ease of buying, but they *also* have an added incentive to act fast and to get even more value from you. This way, you can encourage even more sales than you otherwise could!

Conclusion and Summary

So, there you have it: you now hopefully know everything you could possibly need to know in order to get out there and start selling PLR products. It's an *incredibly* simple business model but only if you are careful to choose the right product and to market it in the right way.

The great thing though is that it will cost you nothing to iterate, test and test again. If your book isn't flying off your digital shelves as you hoped, then you can simply try editing your sales page, or you can try changing your advertising campaign. Maybe you need to lower the price? Maybe you need to throw in more freebies?

Whatever the case, keep on experimenting and tweaking and eventually you'll create something that people are highly excited for and that you'll sell in huge quantities.

And once you've achieved that, you'll have the 'winning formula' you need to get out there and start selling even more eBooks.

You could even use this to buy yourself the time to write your own eBook, or to demonstrate the demand and to refine your technique!

All you need to do, is:

- Find a PLR seller you trust
- Find a product that offers something different and provides good value
- Make sure it includes all the marketing materials you could need
- Purchase the full PLR license
- Make edits that you see fit – match it to your brand, tweak the title and the phrasing as appropriate
- Outsource additional edits if there's anything you can't handle yourself
- Set up your own hosting account with CoolHandles or HostGator
- Get a domain name
- Upload the files
- Create a PayPal 'Buy Now' button
- Add this to the sales page

- Start advertising through Facebook, social media and other channels
- Profit
- Repeat!

With PLR, it couldn't be simpler to keep on adding more products and to keep expanding your earning potential and your audience engagement.

Your days of making measly money through AdSense clicks are over, your days of putting off writing your eBook masterpiece are over. And your days of struggling for hours to create content and marketing materials are over.

Just download, edit, upload, and start to profit!

IMPORTANT: To help you further take action, print out a copy of the *Checklist* and *Mindmap* I provided. You'll also find a Resource Cheat Sheet with valuable sites, posts and articles that I recommend you go through.

Printed by Libri Plureos GmbH in Hamburg,
Germany

9 786069 838198